From Detox to Dignity:

How I Attained and Maintained Sobriety for More than 50 Years

by

LeRoy Bright

The contents of this work, including, but not limited to, the accuracy of events, people, and places depicted; opinions expressed; permission to use previously published materials included; and any advice given or actions advocated are solely the responsibility of the author, who assumes all liability for said work and indemnifies the publisher against any claims stemming from publication of the work.

All Rights Reserved
Copyright © 2022 by LeRoy Bright

No part of this book may be reproduced or transmitted, downloaded, distributed, reverse engineered, or stored in or introduced into any information storage and retrieval system, in any form or by any means, including photocopying and recording, whether electronic or mechanical, now known or hereinafter invented without permission in writing from the publisher.

Dorrance Publishing Co
585 Alpha Drive, Suite 103
Pittsburgh, PA 15238
Visit our website at *www.dorrancebookstore.com*

ISBN: 978-1-6376-4156-9
eISBN: 978-1-6376-4793-6

ABOUT THE AUTHOR

My name is LeRoy Bright, and I was born July 5th, 1930 in Hannibal, Missouri. We had a close-knit family, immediate and extended. My father had been married before meeting my mother and had a son, so we had an older brother who lived with his mother but was at our house as well. He was a great athlete, intelligent, well-versed, and I learned a lot from him. My mother and father had five children, three boys and two girls, I being the oldest. It seemed at times that we were in church a lot, but we learned about God, love, and compassion, which are very valuable qualities. We were happy kids.

As you can see, I was born during the country wide depression with major economic decline and severe unemployment. I never realized that we were poor because we had a nice home, food, clothing, a yard full of chickens, a large garden, and several fruit trees. My father always had a job and worked long hours, and Mom took care of our home. I now realize how difficult that must have been at that time in history.

Going into my senior year, we moved to Muscatine, Iowa for work purposes. I graduated from Muscatine High that year and worked several different jobs. In 1950 we worked construction on the VA Hospital, Iowa City, Iowa. Pay was good, so we drove several miles round trip each work day. Rain often canceled work, so we decided to go to Cedar Rapids, Iowa where factory work was available and was hired that same day. We moved the family to Cedar Rapids shortly thereafter.

In 1951 I went into the Marine Corps and became an Administrative Sergeant in a Cost Accounting Unit. That was the beginning of a great learning experience that has assisted me throughout my life. At some point after discharge, my drinking became atrocious, continously raising its ugly head and remained active until I voluntarily accepted treatment in 1970.

INTRODUCTION/OVERVIEW

Wine-o, drunk, junkie, all these terms have been used synonymously in describing the alcoholic. Alcohol is the drug of choice of more than 100,000,000 of our citizens, and the results are from controlled to extreme uncontrolled. None of us can escape addiction's effect on society. Spiritually, socially, and financially we are all victims of this chemical calamity. Whether or not we care about the alcoholic, we share their consequences. What will we do? Ignore the downtrodden as usual or learn about the illness and try to understand its ramifications and offer quality assistance to family, friends, or whomever instead of often becoming used and manipulated. I am sure we all understand the enabler concept and how we are unwittingly assisting the alcoholic's in their demise and destruction. We are better than that, people!

Many rehabilitation centers need sober volunteers to assist in many areas for which funding is limited. You probably would be pleasantly surprised by the assistance you could offer through the training you would receive.

The following information is offered completely for all persons interested in alcohol use, abuse, and alcoholism. There are a lot of books written on alcoholism, but I hope that we can answer some of your lingering concerns that are often expressed throughout most communities.

The first fact to understand is that we live in a drug-oriented society with many complex parameters, and we will offer specifics on the history, use, and abuse of drug alcohol and the type and availability of treatment and rehabilitation services.

This book will be somewhat different from many others dealing with substance abuse. I do not think that we need a drunk log on how alcoholics arrive at their lowest point in their drinking experiences.

However, since we will be dealing with alcohol and alcoholism, we do need a definition. Alcoholism is a chronic disease affecting the nervous and other internal systems through excessive alcohol consumption. It is like that snake in the grass, seductive and entrails with the ability to kill. We must accept the fact that in the chronic stages of this illness, all mental, physical, and social means have been depleted through the alcoholic's actions or inactions. We find ourselves at the cross roads of life and death. This state of being exposes our incompetence and often results in ostracization (by self or by others).

"FROM DETOX TO DIGNITY"
By Leroy Bright
How I Attained and Maintained Sobriety for More than Fifty Years

"FROM DETOX TO DIGNITY"

I am a recovering alcoholic, sober since the spring of 1970. Recovered and recovering are terms often used synonymously by sober alcoholics. Some would say, and many do, having been sober for fifty years, you have recovered. However, I maintain that it is impossible to recover from an illness (alcoholism) for which there is no cure. Cure in this sense meaning that you could return to social drinking, joining the millions of Americans that seems to never experience problems with alcohol consumption. As long as we maintain sobriety, our illness is arrested, and we can live a normal life and enjoy it. However, it seems that some of us, after a period of sobriety, behave as though we are cured and dare to have that first drink, which cancels all the progress made since your last drink. The old saying that one drink is one too many and 1,000 is never enough will prevail in this case no matter when the next drink is taken, whether through desire or compulsion

Once drinking begins, the compulsion to use becomes all-encompassing and creates a state of powerlessness, which is always stronger than the will not to use. When you have decided to take that first drink, all the effort by yourself and many others in gaining that period of sobriety has vanished. Will power is out the window, and we return to that contemptible, despicable antisocial behavior that we were trying to outlive. What a serious situation we find ourselves in since that first drink. We realize that our tolerance has decreased and our compulsion has increased, leaving us in a very veritable position. Now we are lying damage to our physical, mental, social, and all other aspects of normal everyday living. Sometimes we recognize these changes but choose to continue drinking, which could be very dangerous. At this point, we could be experiencing serious health problems, including but not limited to: DT's, ulcers, cirrhosis of the liver, brain damage, seizures, and several other major health problems.

I awoke on this beautiful spring morning with a lot of sun shining, birds singing but all alone in my Cedar Rapids, Iowa apartment, a city of 109,000 (having lost two good wives to alcoholism). Both of these upstanding ladies tried to help me with my drinking, and it would work for a period of time, but invariably I always returned to a drink and it was off to the races. Alcohol was my constant companion in my darkest days. I had started to realize that my problems were getting more serious.

When I climbed out of bed, I realized that I was dressed in the same clothing that I wore the day before. One of my evaluation tools was the condition of my clothes after a night out. Are they neatly folded on the chair by the bed? If not, my condition is getting worse, by my standards. After a bathroom trip, I made some coffee in the kitchen and took half a mug full (never a full mug in the morning) into the living room to look out and enjoy the sunshine. I was shaky, queasy, and felt rather confused, and this was a different feeling than others I have had, and my concern was heightened. As I sat there looking out the front windows, it began to snow (mind you it is springtime and although it has snowed in the spring but not as a rule). At this time, I began to think about medical problems that I was aware of but never experienced and what was happening to me at this time. I went to the bedroom and killed some wine that was in a half gallon jug. I returned to my seat in the living room. Suddenly the snow began to turn black. Frightening! At this point, I don't know what to do. This snow started to come through the wall. I ran to the bedroom and started to drink some vodka, and that calmed me down somewhat. As I returned to the living room, the snow started to fill the room. I am coming unglued, so I called my sister and brother-in-law and ask for a ride to a treatment center about twenty miles from home. This center was chosen for its reputation for success.

This day I chose to live.

This was not the first time that I had considered getting help. Several other times, when I had a clear thought of seeking help, this thought was clouded by a negative one perpetuated by compulsion or desire to drink, and that is a result of the addictive powers.

My family came right over to transport me to a treatment center about twenty miles from home. I don't remember much about the travel time, the time of day it was, but I do remember how quiet we all were. Very solemn. I think we all had some concerns about my condition. As many years as I had drank, I had never had a serious alcohol related illness, and now D'Ts. This was confirmed by the medical staff at intake.

When we arrived at the center, my brother-in-law went inside and two staff members came out with him and helped me inside. With all of the confusion at the house, we did not call ahead as is the usual procedure, but I was accepted, thank God. After my family provided all the necessary information, I was given a complete physical exam by their doctor, who just happened to be at the center at the time that I was checking in. I don't remember much of what happened the rest of that day or the next. About the third day, I was beginning to participate in all activities.

Later that afternoon, staff informed me that my father had passed from a massive stroke. This was shocking news, although I knew that he was in the hospital other times with minor strokes with little damage.

Plans began immediately to get me back home for two or three days to be with family. My medications were issued to me with specific instructions, and I was back home the next morning.

I was at my sister's house greeting relatives and friends, some I had not seen for several years as they live all across America. My apartment was about four blocks from my sister's house, and I told her about my meds and that I had to go take them. Later back at the house, one of my uncle's drove up and came in carrying a brief case. As we were talking, I ask him about his brief case. We went to a back room, he opened the case, and it was a mini bar. Scotch, gin, and vodka was what it contained. He offered me a drink and I had one, then another.

It was my responsibility to tell him about myself, or to refuse the drinks, realizing that I had just taken my meds. By that third day, I was pretty wasted and I was not going back to treatment. My brother talked to me for a long time, and I finally agreed to go back and he drove me back to the center. The fact was that I was ashamed of my behavior. Staff welcomed me back, and I realized that I needed a lot of help. Those few days home showed me how incapable I am around alcohol.

After a few days back, I emerged and took all that was taught in all groups very seriously. I learned to use unlimited conceptualization, visualizing how wonderful sobriety (complete freedom in all aspects) could really be. I promised myself to capitalize on every learning experience each and every day, whether or not it applied to me at that time.

Train the mind, and the body must follow. It's like a computer that prints whatever is contained in the memory bank. This positive mind set must include a total recall of all the absolute asinine behavioral conduct displayed over the years with serious consequence for the alcoholics and all those around them. As I recalled all of the abuse to my body, mind, spirit, and soul, I was in the process of mentally killing the old man with a new positive approach to life. I NOW THINK OF THE MAN THAT WALKED INTO THIS CENTER LOOKING LIKE ME. All HIS NEGITIVE LIFE STYLE, I LEAVE HERE BECAUSE THE NEW ME CANNOT AFFORD THE OLD MAN BECAUSE I WANT TO LIVE A HAPPY LIFE.

I was continually impressed by the exuberance with which the counselors, group leaders, doctors, nurses, and other staff members seemed to have in assisting us however they could. I wanted to experience that feeling and the ability to help others, but it was just a passing thought. My subconscious mind was obviously active as we will see later.

I have always realized that we all desire two very important components in our lives: love and happiness. We try various methods of reaching those goals, and some are successful and some are never completely attained, but the basic motives remain consistent.

After three weeks of intensive program activities, it seemed that I always had three or four of my classmates in my room at free time, of course the door was always open. They all wanted to talk about their lives not being very good and everything else about drugs and alcohol. Maybe they wanted to talk with me because I was somewhat older. I found out that they wanted to be sober without doing the work. There are no short cuts, and this turned into motivational secessions, but they keep coming back. I must have said something that stuck, and I prayed a lot.

A couple weeks later, one of our doctors called me into her office and said that she wanted to talk to me about the people in my room and that she had talked to some of them. I thought that I was in some serious trouble. I told her that I sort of steered them in the right direction, and they answered most of their own questions. She then asked if I had ever considered becoming a counselor, and at this time I had not thought much about it. However, I have always been a people person. I quietly observe personalities, interpersonal relationships, and all aspects of human behavior. It is interesting.

A week later, we talked again about counseling, and after some thought, it began to sound like something I might enjoy. She said that she thought I might be effective.

I was not aware that she was pulling together resources that would assist me in my endeavors. I don't know exactly how many weeks I was at the center because I count progress as ongoing. Instinctively I realized that it was time to leave, as I had soaked up the very best information offered, and I will recall various aspects for a lifetime. At checkout the doctor gave me a list of instructions to follow when I got home.

At home I had three meetings, and each played a part in the final program that was agreed on. However, I was most impressed by a brother from one large church that had a lot of input and knowledgeable about community problems. I was provided an office, phone, and supplies in a community center. We decided that an outreach program would be the entry into the client base because these are the people I drank with some time ago. I was concerned about my acceptance of those that really needed help and the larger community. After a few tests, they realized that I was sober and giving my best, day or night. This church group became my sponsoring entity in the community.

My outreach work was very demanding, in that I made house calls, counseled, transported clients to treatment, and assisted them in the social areas as well. The needs assessment connected the client to the necessary community service assistance program. I received a call from a family member stating that a friend needed help. When I arrived at his house, I found him to be in bad physical condition. In bed, unable to stand or function very well, but still asking for a drink, and his friends were giving it to him. That's what drinking buddies do. I explained his condition to him and his friends and ask them to get him up dressed and presentable as I was taking him to the hospital at 1 P.M. Of course he said that he did not want to go to any hospital.

When I returned at 1 P.M., they had him up and dressed, but he did not want to go, nor did he realize how sick he was. They got him into the car and we took off. He was very quiet and soon he had passed out. We got him checked into the unit at the hospital and I left. Three days later, the doctor from the hospital called and said that I had gotten him there in time to possibly save his life as he may not have lived through that first night. Upon discharge he was a changed man and cut way back on his drinking but never completely quit.

As I was interacting with many different types of people, I realized that many of them were having problems, and some were not drug related. After being in several homes having various problems, I thought that it was time to develop a night group meeting at the center that would welcome everyone that chose to come, regardless of their concerns. Thursday nights were chosen, starting at 7 P.M. until all had their opportunity to speak. We used several guidelines, including some from AA, NA, the Bible, etc. This program was of special interest to my wife, Nellie J. Bright, who took over a lot of the planning and program content. She had some great ideas to keep it real by introducing something fresh each week.

My wife Nellie was a wonderful lady, very intelligent, talented, Christian, great designer/seamstress, and one of the most insightful person that treated everyone from the heart and made us all feel special. A beautiful person that was recovering as I was, so we did it together for forty-three years. I can truthfully say that she has recovered since passing away August 15th, 2013.

Regardless of what situation was presented by members of the group, someone through camaraderie and compassion seemed to have an acceptable answer; if not we would do research of the topic for the correct answer. Members of the group, given the responsibility of selecting a name, came up with The Nitty Gritty Group.

NELLIE J. BRIGHT 1924-2013

Upon discharge from treatment, I was visiting an old friend who did not drink. As we were talking, a lady dropped in to say hello to my friend, and it was a lady I had met before. She had to leave but promised to meet with me the next afternoon.

Over a pot of coffee, we talked about everything for almost three hours. She was recently divorced and shared time with their three children. We started dating, and a few months later, were married. 1970 was a good year.

She was a beautiful lady both mentally and physically and deserves to be remembered for having the ability to make those with which she came into contact feel special, and we all felt number one.

I dedicate this book in her memory, without whom this might never have been written.

She always said, "Be well versed in your area of expertise, able to give a quality answer to all questions ask."

It was a great forty-three years, and bless her heart she has recovered.

She has recovered.

WHAT A COMPLETE
CHRONIC STATE!

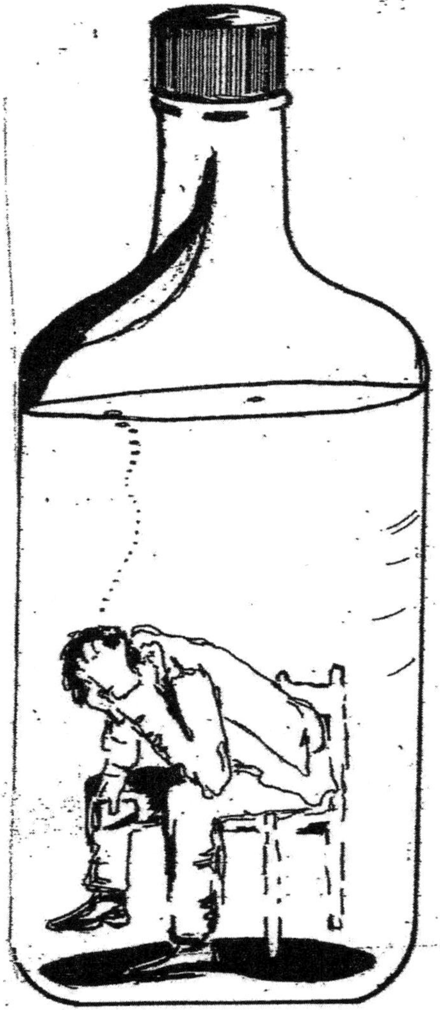

HAVE YOU BOTTLED YOUR
WAY TO THE BOTTOM?

HEARING RELEVANT
INFORMATION AGAIN,
STARTING TO LISTEN.

LISTENING

STANDING, AT-
TEMPTING TO
EMERGE MENTALLY.

SLOWLY ACCEPTING

FINALLY GETTING
SERIOUS.

ESCAPING
MENTAL CLEANSING

TOSSING STONE,
BREAKING BOTTLE
DEPICTING KILLING
THE OLD MAN/WOMAN
FREEING ONESELF FROM
THE ALCOHOLISM SYN-
DROME TO WORK ON
PERSONAL GROWTH.

OUR SOBER YEARS

Our sobriety was approached as a necessary part of our lives. It was something we never discussed after a good laugh at our stupidity when we began dating. I think that whenever you can look back and accept all your faults, clam them, file them away, and start to kill the old person, you create the new you that has empathy for your fellow man, which allows you to see clearly.

You enjoy family, friends, and home life, and you do all the honest, Christian, upstanding things that sober folks automatically do, and there is no substitute for clean living. The reward is in doing.

As you are aware by now, I have mentioned some of Nellie's talents. Here is an example of a young Nellie Akers.

NELLIE AKERS, fifteen, Kirksville, Missouri, won the Fox Midwest "Search for Talent" contest at the Kennedy theater, recently in Moberly, Missouri. She was the only colored among twelve other contestants. Nellie has won several contests in Kirksville with her imitation of Mae West. As winner of the Fox contest, she went to Kansas City for the state contest, the winner of which received an expense-paid trip to Hollywood, the film capital. In this last contest, Nellie sang the blues. She is the daughter of Mrs Pearl Lawson, 315 East Elm street Kirksville, Missouri.

TRAINING

During one of our weekly meetings, my sponsoring group informed me that two educational opportunities had been established for me as had previously been discussed. The first was starting in two weeks at MHI, one of the mental health institutes substance abuse programs that was highly rated throughout the state of Iowa and beyond, due to Iowa Governor Harold Hughes declaring that he was a recovering alcoholic and doing what he could for treatment programing. The other program was a new one-year study at one of the universities to begin January of the following year.

During this time, everything was moving very fast, so I had to slow down and check my personal inventory to make sure that I remembered that sobriety is a way of life, self-controlled, sane, and devoid of alcoholic beverages and illicit drugs. You learn to enjoy a complete positive mental and physical status, and adjustments are made where change is mandatory. Replacing all negative thoughts with positive actions becomes a way of life.

On the designated Monday morning, I arrived at MHI and met the staff that I would train under. I was impressed by one nurse and two therapist whose names I was aware of but had never met before. Their reputations for innovative and effective treatment modalities was well known. My first week of training was reading, retaining, and being tested on several books on counseling, therapy, and interpersonal relationships. They also provided me a detailed outline of program structure, components, etc. They managed to keep me busy.

After a couple weeks, I had done pretty well on the materials that I was presented, so I was scheduled to shadow the counselors as they did their one on one, small and large group sessions and paper work.

I was also having classes on budget preparation and management, grants writing, hiring and supervision of personnel.

At the end of the third week, I was off and drove home for the weekend to be with my wife. When I returned to MHI, they had given me one of the offices to work from. They also informed me that I would have participatory involvement in all groups. However, I was not aware that I would have some of the responsibility for one on one sessions with the non-compliant clients. This was my test.

As the morning session began, I noticed a lot of new faces and was told that while I was at home, there was a graduation. We now have a different group of people. Some were attentive, some were distant, some were disgusted, and some wanted to leave (especially those sent through the court system).

We worked with everyone getting them actuated to the program concept. They also participated in AA, NA, and other important meetings on campus as well as out in the general community. This program gets positive results, teaching that there must be an attitude change from within, reflecting on your life family, past behavior, and striving to make positive change. The mind is a positive organ, and treated well, it will deliver.

My six weeks of training are over, and it's time to return home with renewed motivation. Very happy to see my wife and be back to work with this new energy and mental expansiveness and a significantly effective program policy.

After being back on the job for almost two weeks, my wife's sister called with an invitation for us to spend Christmas with her in Ohio. We thought that it might be good to get out of town for a while, so I made arrangements at work to be off for two weeks. We left for Ohio a little before Christmas and had a good trip, although it had snowed, but the roads were clear.

Her sister and some of her friends greeted us on our arrival, and it was a joyous time. Sister was a famous Christian gospel singer, song writer, publisher, arranger, and teacher. One of her good friends was a young minister from her church, and we seemed to have a lot in common. I was active in the church, so we had a lot to talk about. After two days of good food, good conversation, and relaxation, I was beginning to wonder how complete the substance abuse programing was in this community. By this time, every one of Sister's friends knew what I did for a living, so they invited me to speak after church services on the first Sunday morning that we were in town. At the appointed time, I gave a general overview of the alcohol abuse problem in Americans stating that at any given time, more than 10,000,000 are affected. It is a vicious disease that destroys millions of lives in America and is more destructive among the poor because of the limitations poverty imposes on its captives.

The second question was from a lady that explained that her company received a large contract, and the executives decided to reward the employees with a celebration on the last three hours of the last Friday of that month. There were about eighty people in attendance, and there was plenty food, drinks, both alcoholic and non-alcoholic, music. A good time for all. She explained that one man that worked closely with her was very quiet on the job but a very good worker. It seemed that he was the only one of the group intoxicated, and I thought he must be an alcoholic. My conclusion was based on previous home observations (my uncle was an alcoholic).

I later learned that two young ladies were responsible for coercing him into taking his first drink, and he has never had a drink since. How wrong can you be? So how do you tell the difference between a drunk person and the alcoholic? Not by sight alone, as you have learned. The most accurate disclosures we have are the intake processes by substance abuse programs, hospitals, doctors' offices, and other medical facilities. That is where some insight into a person's history is revealed. There were several more questions, and after one hour, the meeting was completed.

As we were leaving, one of the young men came up and asked if I would be interested in visiting some of the treatment programs in the city. We were thinking along the same lines, and he picked me up the next afternoon. The first stop was the city health departments substance abuse program. I met with the director, and he was impressed with some of my insight He said that he would like to hire me, but there were no funds available. He said that in his opinion, Iowa programing was somewhat ahead of Ohio. He referred me to another program after making a phone call and talking to the director about our meeting. She was able to meet with me the next morning at 10 a.m.

I met the director of the substance abuse program at her office the next morning, and it was a pleasure. We talked about everything that we knew about alcohol, alcohol abuse, alcoholism, and treatment. We also discussed our personal addictions, treatment, and sobriety. This lady was very intelligent with three years of law school, until alcohol and drugs took over. She offered me a job as one of the counselors on part-time bases due to budget restraints, however a new budget year begins in two months, and funds will be available. I accepted the offer and was happy that my wife would be close to her sister. I was to report for duty in thirty days.

This program was part of an umbrella agency operating a variety of programs, including head start, food buying club, credit union, manpower training, employment opportunities, senior citizens, and nutrition assistance. The agency was an advocate for the poor and an agent of social change. I came into the center the next day and met all the staff and observed some of their work. They were all recovering alcoholics and seemed good at their jobs.

Well, time has come for us to return home and start to plan our move to Ohio. The results of our trip were very rewarding, something I had not expected. I had to meet with my supervisors and offer my resignation explaining my new opportunities. They seemed to accept that I would be moving on at some point, so this became my last week with this group.

We began to consider what part of our belongings we wanted to take to Ohio. We tried to be selective and cover our daily needs. We decided to take our kitchen appliances, bedroom furniture, washer-dryer, entertainment equipment, clothing, and two easy chairs from the living room. Most of the rest we sold, and the balance was donated to a community help program. We rented the appropriate size trailer, and after several days, got it loaded. It became time for us to get our financial matters in order and bid farewell to family and friends to begin our 600-mile drive to Ohio.

Two days earlier, Sister called and said that she was giving us a present and for us to come directly to her place. When we arrived, she presented us with a key to one of the apartments in her building. This was a new building in a great neighborhood, and although we were very appreciative of the gift, we had to explain that we could not afford to live there. She had paid all expenses for the first two months and had to explain our situation to the owner, who returned her money which she passed on to us.

When we were visiting over Christmas, we had dinner at a couple's apartment that we met from church and we really enjoyed the evening. We happened to meet the manager and spoke briefly as we were leaving and told him that we would be moving to town in about thirty days. We thought that this would be a good time to call that manager asking about vacancies he may have. We were blessed to get the last two-bedroom apartment available. It was a safe place, and the rent was reasonable. We got all moved in and had our first good night's rest in our new home. I had two days before reporting to work, so we drove around the city, trying to get the lay of the land. Later Sister called, came by, and took us to dinner. She did not like to cook, so she liked to frequent the better restaurants in the city.

My first day on the job went well, trying to introduce myself (by phone) to the contact people of the various agencies that we used on behalf of our clients. Later that day, I went out and met some of these people and got a feel for what they did. At our center, I met five of our sober clients that came in each day and offered support to some that were not doing well. They were always positive and willing to provide a ride when appropriate. The next day, I sat in on a group session, traveled with a team member on an outreach call, and had two new clients. After a short period of time, I had established a case load. I was really enjoying my job, although I could not get it done part-time, but it didn't matter as I was seeing change in my clients. I felt so good being sober that I wanted everyone sober, but I knew that was not reality.

The day was coming to an end, and a lady client whom had been sober for almost eight months (I was told) asked to speak with me in my office. She wanted to talk about her husband, whom she said has a serious problem with alcohol. He misses some work on his construction job where he is a foreman with lots of responsibility. She is concerned about the possibility of him losing his job after more than twenty years.

I told her that I would like to meet her husband as soon as possible, and she informed me that he will not talk to anyone because he does not need help, does not have a problem, and has his drinking under control. She stated that she comes in for counseling Tuesday and Thursday afternoons, and I suggested we figure a way to get him into the center.

I do not know how she got him into the center, but one day there he was. She introduced us and went down the hallway to her appointment with her counselor. Her husband and I talked about everything on earth for almost one hour, except drinking. We established a free relationship and scheduled a meeting for the next afternoon. When he came in, we talked about his drinking, his family, and his job. He got very honest about his life and said that he needed help and wanted to change his behavior. We talked about treatment including AA, and I asked if he would attend a meeting with me at 7 P.M. that night. I thought the AA program would fit with his work schedule as there are A.M. and P.M. meetings. When we arrived at the meeting, he was a little tentative at first as this was his first meeting, but after hearing several speakers, he also had something to say and enjoyed being there. He and his wife attended some meetings together and some alone by choice. It was their way of getting their meetings in around their busy schedules. They worked hard on their program and was staying sober and started to regain much of what was lost when both drinking. They were back in church, had a copy of Alcoholics Snonymous and the twelve steps and twelve traditions, and they used them all.

The second week that I was there, the director called me in and we talked about the program. She asked me what I thought we needed, and I said an education coordinator to help bring staff up another level. She thought this was a great idea and told me to go back to my area and write a proposal for the job, which would be mine if funded. She gave me an outline of technical information that must be included, but the narrative, budget, and other particulars is up to you. When you finish, we will go over it and get it submitted.

That was the first time that I had the responsibility of writing a technical document, and she only needed to make a few corrections to complete it. She was very intelligent and studied law for three years before alcohol took over, and I learned a lot from her. She had been sober for several years and was a very positive person.

Several weeks later, the grant was funded, and I now had some more work to do, as I wanted to keep working my caseload as well. We thought it would be advantageous if I used the Thursday afternoon staff meetings for educational information and anytime that I had opportunity to assist. I was remembering some of the things I learned about while training in Iowa at one of the Mental Health Institutes Alcoholism Programs. They were talking about counselor certification and program accreditation. It all seemed so very far in the future. As time passed, I began to hear more about the certification of counselors. I reviewed the work of all our counselors to find our weak spots and help to strengthen the area of need. I realized that there would be some future time when we would have to be concise concerning the knowledge of our jobs. Some of the areas that needed assistance were intake and evaluation, individual, group, and family counseling, referral, record keeping, reporting, and outreach, plus several closely related areas.

Specifically I found that we also needed more training in sensitivity, group therapy awareness, understanding of self, and relationships with others. Establishing a positive social culture is very important. We must remember that we are always greater than those sometimes static conditions in which we find ourselves from time to time.

After a few months, the Director called me in and told me that she had other interest and would be resigning and asked if I would like to compete for her job. Of course I was interested, and her job was posted by the agency and she recommended me to the selection committee. By this time, I was well-known throughout the agency, and my work ethic was well-established. Finally I was awarded the position of director of the alcoholism program by the agency CEO. I was surprised how much he knew about me as we talked about all the changes I expected to make. The first order of business was to find a rental that we could afford to move our central alcoholism drop-in center out of the agency facilities. We found a spot in the heart of the drug and alcohol area, and the owner gave us a real break on the rent. As he stated, we need you working in this area. After moving in and posting our identifying information on the outside of the building, we were open.

I now had the responsibility for proposal development and implementation. This necessitated grants writing, budget preparation and management, hiring, training and supervision of staff. I thought that it was time to upgrade our goals and objectives.

The overall program objective is the initiation and maintenance of sobriety of the alcoholic poor, so that he/she/family may mobilize their resources and utilize the neighborhood service system and all other community resources conducive to rehabilitation of the family unit. The nature of services provided is a varied approach to the physical, mental, and social problems presented by the alcoholic and his/her family, including out-reach/intervention into the cycle of alcohol abuse, intake, counseling, group therapy, evaluation, referral/placement, follow-up, and community education.

Our program assists primarily the alcoholic poor whom are suffering from both poverty and alcoholism.

One of the continuing responsibilities I now have is fund raising. The community need is always greater than our budget abilities, so we are continuously seeking new sources.

I found that HEW had a slate of speakers (some famous) that were available to their locally funded programs for fund raising purposes. We requested a certain person from the list of speakers and was blessed to get a great pitcher for the LA Dodgers to come in for a weekend. We had TV, radio slots, large personal meetings, and large public affairs that were quite successful. He was a really great guy, a people person that left a lot of happy people with some relative information. My wife and I entertained him in our home, and the experience will never be forgotten.

During one of the community meetings, he reminded parents of their tremendous responsibility in the type education their children receive, including scholastic, Christian, and drug education. In a home where there are no clear boundaries, ambivalence is the usual results. Simply meaning that a simultaneous attraction toward and a repulsion from the use of alcoholic beverages. The inability to make a positive choice, through lack of knowledge, could be damaging in their future. We have found that environment has a great influence on the behavior of young people. They pick up the positive as well as the negative, so you can no longer tell your children to do as you say and not as you do.

He stated that in most communities, some of these listed treatment programs exist. Alcoholism Anonymous, community hospitals, community substance and chemical abuse programs, private agencies and organizations, physicians, veteran's administration, and other social and religious organizations and individuals in your telephone directory.

I previously stated that all human service programs find that funding is always less than the existent need. However, I was able through considerable innovation, ingenuity, and resourcefulness to pull together previously unavailable community resources to strengthen our program. Through our annual program review, these special funds continued.

As funds became available, we rented a building on the south side and opened The South-End Drop-In Center. We also rented space in one of the larger community centers, giving us three areas of operation. We were able to staff those centers with a chief counselor and all other staff as necessary. The goal is to provide the same complete services offered at Central Drop-In Center at the new facilities.

Our client case load was a combination of people from across the spectrum with specific racial/cultural differences, but our experienced staff soon had all on the same page. The goal has always been striving to end the misery of alcoholism and return to a normal life through sobriety.

It has been demonstrated to the community in many places that these highly apathetic, socially alienated, ostracized individuals can be rehabilitated. When the family situation is explored, we often find child neglect, abuse, physical defects, and emotional problems. An alcoholic parent is an irresponsible parent and often neglect simple medial measures. Through studies made of family problems, we find that it does little good to attempt rehabilitation of the alcoholic without complete family involvement. Through this family involvement, many general health problems are detected, and referrals are made to the proper agencies. Continued follow-up and supportive therapy are essential to the alcoholic for sustained sobriety. In summary the ability to motivate an individual to positive constructive change, and to instill a sense of responsibility, is necessary and must be exemplified in order that rehabilitation might occur.

Along with accomplishing these goals, education is a major part of our process, and to that end, we continue our weekly in-house progress sessions. All present staff members have completed training at Central States Training Institute of Addictions, Chicago, Illinois, and Alcoholism Studies at Ohio Dominican College, Columbus, Ohio. Our educational literature designed for every segment of the community was revised to include the latest on alcohol abuse and alcoholism.

After the move, our Central Drop-in Center became a facility that the community utilized and identified with and became the hub of our evening program activities, including A.A., Al-Anon, family counseling, rap sessions, staff meetings, advisory council meetings, etc. After a few months with additional staff, we were able to open the center on Saturdays, staffed by two members of our crew. It provided a safe place for some clients to share coffee and sober conversations. They were also able to work through their problems with the counselors.

We found it important to establish a program component that would be encompassing for our clients in various stages of rehab/sobriety that needed something to call their own. This would be a client supported organization comprised of enthusiastic motivated persons whose goal is to get sober and to stay sober. The rules and regulations are those created by clients that now come to the center instead of going to the bar. The total alcoholism peer group program was approved by the drop-in center program director. High lights were those members showing individual dignity and pride, in their quest for sobriety and life style changes. As more of our clients became sober, the incentive became a desire to be included in the alcoholism peer group.

This becomes a very important group for many single members with time on their hands and financial stability through SSI or some other means. It was also a method of intervention to be used by the center staff when necessary. From this peer group, several members became job ready, and three were employed within the community. Sobriety is a reward in itself, but the benefits are undeniable.

The inter value of counseling is to see the gradual positive change in a client's mental and physical stability. When one often finds for the first time (in some cases) that a sober life can be normal, happy, and productive, it opens many avenues.

Unfortunately there are some for which sobriety is not a goal. When we realize this fact, it is our responsibility to provide quality service to the individual for as long as they participate. The end results are often a reduction in daily consumption leading to perhaps extending one's life.

Fast forward to 1978 and the completion of the alcoholism counselor's certification board. The effectiveness of the board was well-recieved, giving counselors recognition and pride in their work.

The following statement is taken directly from the boards booklet and states, "The certification process in Ohio will facilitate the recognition of alcoholism counseling as a profession in the health-care field."

The following are some of the professional tasks of the alcoholism counselor as defined by the board. Intake/evaluation, assisting in developing a treatment plan, individual and group counseling, crisis intervention, reporting and record keeping, outreach, client education, and staff training among other tasks.

Our complete staff qualified for certification under the grand personing process that was based upon prior full-time paid and supervised work experience that would be good for two years, after which time re-certification would have to be accomplished through regular processes.

What are the regular processes in re-certification? The basic requirements and conditions for the professional standard used in the Ohio certification program are those that deal with skills, knowledge, and attitudes, along with the demonstrated ability to perform the professional tasks of the alcoholism counselor, some of which are listed above. Alcoholism counseling is a discrete professional service involving a primary commitment to the welfare and care of the client and the possession of special knowledge, skills, and competencies.

Each applicant must provide evidence of competencies in the following areas: Basic communication skills, knowledge of alcohol use and alcoholism, prevention, treatment, and rehabilitation. Evaluation and assessment. Referral skills. Case finding and counseling and treatment. The counseling and treatment processes relate to the primary direct delivery of service.

Our program is on solid financial footing, and all staff members are certified. The next adjustment will be the upcoming program accreditation.

As time moved on, my wife was having a difficult time driving around the city to visit her sister, shopping, etc., as she has never liked large cities. Her youngest daughter came for a visit, liked it, and decided to stay with us for a while. I was happy because my wife was happy, and there was always a lot of laughter, joking around, and fun times. Daughter enrolled in college to complete work on her degree. During this time, she earned her income from a modeling gig at which she was very successful, until she lost interest after college. She worked several different jobs, but I think she enjoyed finance and all its challenges the most. Sometime later she moved back to Iowa, had a son, and developed a successful child care program that served many children.

My wife and I was doing some serious talking about our future. As we were aging, social security for both of us would not be what we wanted to depend on. So we decided to take some time off, go home, and see what might be available with benefits. I submitted my resume to two companies. I heard back from one, had an interview, set up a future start time of thirty days. Now that I was committed, the next thirty days will be busy.

Back in OHIO, we had several things to take care of, starting with talking to my staff and writing my resignation and meeting with various clients that I have known for several years. I also had to take care of some small bills, get our home sold, and tie up other loose ends. I really will miss going to the center each work day as I had for over nine years, seeing and being with staff and clients. I learned that counseling when properly administered could be a learning experience for all concerned, remembering that the client is always the greatest beneficiary.

I went to the agency office for a meeting with the Director of Operations to discuss my resignation. He was not happy to see me go and tried to see if I would change my mind. We had a lengthy conversation, and he understood how important returning to Iowa was to me and my family, and we parted on good terms. He said that he would send in the Special Projects Director and I should familiarize him with program specifies. I know this person, and he is a good guy and has a reputation for getting the job done. He will oversee the program and staff until a new director has been hired. I had four months' salary remaining in this budget year, and I chose to receive it monthly at our home in Iowa. One other concern was selling our home, however we were lucky to have a friend that is a realter. He arranged our buy, now he can arrange our sale. He is completely trustworthy.

The day came when we were to leave for Iowa. We were a day ahead of the movers with the truck. When we were there a few weeks ago, friends invited us to dinner at their home in a mobile home park. The grounds were very well-maintained. I was impressed as I had never been in a mobile home park or a mobile home before. After talking to our friends, we thought we should look into the mobile home market as an immediate temporary shelter since the financial arrangements seemed appealing and our home had not yet sold. Friends drove us to the sales agency the next day. We saw many homes on the lot and we were in and out of several until we saw one that we really liked. It had what we were looking for, so we bought it. The agency had responsibility for delivering the unit on time to our designated lot, set it up, and hook up all necessary utilities. We were located in the adult section, and the agency had completed all the work, making our home livable. We picked up our keys from the office and found everything complete.

We looked forward to seeing that large truck with all our belongings the next afternoon. We still had time now to decide on the placement of various pieces from our house that's on the truck.

The truck arrived on time and was unloaded, and everything found its place inside. We did have some things not needed at this time, so out to the shed they went. The shed was left by some former tenants, and I am thankful. Now that things were in place, it began to look like home and feel like home. Our family and friends visited often, and sometimes I think it was the novelty of the place as none of us had ever experienced this type of living before. We enjoyed living here because it was very well-maintained, and everyone kept their areas neat and clean. Our neighbors were friendly and engaging, as was the office manager and staff. If a personal problem arose, they were quick to offer a satisfactory resolution to the situation, making it a peaceful place to live

The day for me to report to work on my new job was finally here. I was assigned to the coal crew. This was physical labor, and it felt good for a change. It took a couple days to learn from the old guys how to work the equipment and save your back whenever possible. Our responsibility (stated simply) was to make sure that the overhead bunkers were always full of coal, used to feed the furnaces, turn the generators, and produce electrical power.

One Monday morning, we all got a surprise when we reported to our work station. We had a new crew member, and she was female, and this was the first time that a woman was assigned to our crew. As we started to get acquainted, she stated how satisfied she was to be working with us and liked being outside in the air. She also had to practically beg to get outside and became one of the hardest workers on our crew.

I had been there almost five years when I started to hear about lay-offs coming soon. I realized that my time at the company would not survive a layoff, so I started to look again for what might be available throughout the community.

I contacted that second company, and surprisingly I had an interview, was hired, and to start work in three days. I reported on time and was assigned as a utility person. We had a crew of six with the responsibility for checking and cleaning circuit boards. We worked well together, had a lot of fun, worked a lot of overtime, and finished everything on time. We worked harmoniously. Anytime I had a few minutes slack time, I was over in the inspection section trying to learn something new about that job. I had two friends that wanted to teach me all they could, time permitting. There was a great deal of technical information to be reserved. Over time I was taught a lot about the job and things to prepare me if ever I had the opportunity to be tested.

After more than a year, a posting for inspector was signed by several people, including myself. Testing was scheduled for all on the list. I did very well on the test and was blessed to get the job. A major part of my new job consisted of my assurance that all parts that I inspected were in tolerance according to the specs. I had three different computer programs to work from, so findings were exact. If not correct, parts were sent back to the mill for necessary adjustments. This job was always interesting.

At home one evening, I began to reflect on my sobriety and how many changes were necessary early on. Initially I had to read each label on products to make sure they were alcohol free. I made my own cough syrup, and whatever else was not suitable was eliminated.

My faith in our Lord, and Savior Jesus Christ helped me over the rough spots and one of my memory verses is 2 Tim 2:15, "Study to shew thyself approved unto God, a workman that needeth not to be ashamed, righty dividing the word of truth." I am not advocating that my methods are the only ones that work as we are all individuals, but we must always remember that practice makes permanent.

After several months, our relator called with an offer that was practically our asking price, so we accepted, and the deal was completed. We now began to look for a house with a garden spot. We looked at several houses and finally settled on a large two-story with a large back yard with plenty garden area. One thing that made the trade of our mobile home toward the house was that the salesman had in the past sold mobile homes, so he understood the value of the trade, and I think he may have had a sale in mind.

Two years later, we were made aware that a house we had some interest in was back on the market. We liked this house because it was all on one floor, had a large garden area, large front porch, and the rear porch had been converted into a room. This served us well, but we realized that it was a little small when traveling family came to visit. About three years later, we purchased a three-bedroom newer house, which remains our permanent home. The smaller house would become a rental for almost twenty years. Over time I did a lot of repairs, including bathroom, paint, replace hot water tank, furnace, roof and siding, etc.

The years really seemed to fly by, and its 1995, and I think it is time to retire. Time to slow down and enjoy some of my other leisure activities. Instead my wife had a few things for me to work on. With her list and me working on the rental, I had not worked this hard in years, but I finally finished. Now I was bored. We had traveled considerably early on, and now the road did not seem exciting. We settled into daily routines and had a lot of good times. I sat around for about a year trying to think of something to do that I found interesting. Mentally I always seem to revert back to some form of substance abuse assistance. I still wanted to work with alcoholics on a part-time basis with less counseling responsibility. I made a couple calls, submitted my resume, and received an appointment for an interview the next morning.

I met this very knowledgeable lady that interviewed me and explained where I might fit in since I did not agree to all shift times. So she hired me for the on-call position, which was ideal. I worked 7-3:30, 2-10:30, and 3-11:30. The good thing was that your monthly schedule was always made available to you, so you could plan your activities accordingly. I usually worked between nine and sixteen days a month, which kelp me involved, plus gives me a lot of time at home. I worked adult recovery or DD recovery clients. It did not matter to me which group I worked with because they all had a personal responsibility in learning to listen and not just hear. If all they ever did was to hear the word and not listen, they will be worse with no benefit. When we listen, you mull it around in your mind and utilize all the positive aspects of it, file it away, for some day you will need it.

We had the responsibility for making sure clients were at their appointed activities on time. Sometimes this would mean transporting them to the YMCA, AA, NA, or other meetings and affairs as scheduled. All your work had to be correctly documented on each client you worked with. When working in the center, you were confronted by clients wanting/needing something at all times. After a period of time, I enjoyed the different shift changes as it gave time to meet and work with other staff members.

In 2013 my wife was not feeling great at times, and I hated to leave her. The sicker she got, the less I worked. She was diabetic and had high blood pressure, and we had her in the hospital several times, and she always seemed better for a while. I retired again (for the last time) sometime in June, made it official July 1st, 2013. I believe she was starting to suffer mini strokes. We had hospice service, and they are wonderful people, caring, knowledgeable, compassionate, Christian, and just great at what they do. We got her back to the hospital for a respite, and she passed a few days later. I do not think that she was in pain as they had a good pain management system in place. I thank God for that. This was a sad time for us all; it's that place you have no control over and you are a little lost from reality.

TAXES/REHAB/FUNDING

The rehab treatment facilities in every community dealing with alcoholism and other drug problems should offer a quality program available to all that need assistance, regardless of financial status. Funding is a very critical component that often determines the scope of services, staff, and quality of treatment modalities. This difficulty should not exist because tax dollars derived from alcohol production should/could be more equitably dispensed.

However, what we have are career politicians and politically ambitious regulatory bureaucrats work from an administrative system in which the need to follow complex procedures impedes effective action and eliminates any opportunity for a difference of opinion. They impose strict standards, quality control procedures, and governmental economic policies, which are usually unfair. Taxes always seem to run disproportionately up hill.

The foregoing statements were based on the flow of tax dollars from the governments tight control of the alcohol beverage industry and the distribution of those funds. When I explore the system that's in place, let's look at three categories.

First is the more than 100,000,000 Americans that use alcohol on special occasions several times a year, including holidays, birthdays, industry functions, etc. These affairs being rather unique often served the most expensive drinks, including champagne. A great deal of tax dollars are generated from this group. The second group are the heavy drinkers, not as large but individual consumption is much higher. Most drink daily and spend money that should go to family support. Home life becomes unpleasant, running out of excuses at work, mental resolve to do better fails time after time. Finally loses job, and each one thereafter is a little less important than the one you just lost.

The third group are the practicing alcoholics that spend all of their money on alcohol. They work when they can, beg, steal, and manipulate to provide that all important alcoholic beverage. This is a vicious disease that destroys millions of lives. To the poor, the disease is even more destructive because of the limitations poverty imposes on its captives

I am trying to point out the disparity between taxes collected on alcohol sales and those allocated to alcohol treatment programs. All legal alcohol manufactured in America by distillation or fermentation is controlled by the governmental authority. We must remember that at one time this, chronic alcoholic was perhaps in stages one and two above. No one is born an alcoholic.

When a barrel of whiskey is manufactured, processed, distributed, and finally reaches community stores for retail sales, it has been systematically taxed along the way. A more equitable statist earmarked tax allocation would end the gravy train for those that derive benefits from alcohol taxes but have nothing at all to do with the end results of alcoholism. What a travesty.

I vividly recall in the 1970's an organization, for which I worked in Ohio, presented in person a proposal to the Ohio House requesting one cent of each tax dollar collected from the retail sale of alcoholic beverages to be shared by all programs having received state accreditation. They listened and said that they would reply in two weeks.

In less than two weeks, we had their response, which was no stated several different ways through reams of paper. I am sure there are other efforts made with similar results. This is another glaring example of our government at work.

FACT SHEET ON ALCOHOLISM

It is cunning, baffling, complex, progressive, treacherous, deceitful, seductive, and entrapping in its three phases of illness, including sociological, psychological, and physiological dimensions.

Did you know that 3 to 5 percent of the employed male population are in trouble with alcohol, and the problem started six to eight years before becoming obvious.

That it is a family illness, and the Public Health Service classified it as the third most serious health problem in our country at the time.

Skid Row (a place where the pompous gloat as they pass by) is comprised of only 3 percent of the alcoholic population. I wonder where the 97 percent are? You guessed it, homes, offices, factories, and places where normal people gather.

This is a vicious disease that destroys millions of lives in America. To the poor, the disease is even more destructive because of the limitations poverty imposes on its captives.

1 Pet 1:13, "Wherefore gird up the loins of your mind, be sober, and hope to the end for the grace that is to be brought unto you at the revelation of Jesus Christ."

ALCOHOLIC CONFUSION

I arrived to work the afternoon shift and was informed by the female counselor at the desk that a man escorted in by police, became very belligerent after they had left. He refused to comply with the in-take or other necessary procedures, so they escorted him to his room to cool off. I went down to his room to talk to him and maybe offer some assistance toward behavior modification. The door was open so I stepped inside with my hand extended so he inadvertently shook it. I explained to him that everyone at the center was subject to all the rules and regulations or requested to leave regardless of how they arrived.

We finlly got around to talking about him and he brought up his father. He stated that his father beat him when he was drunk (which was often) and I hated him. I ask if his father lived in the local community, he said that his father passed several years ago. You are allowing a dead man to control your life. I suggest you forgive your father (for your own stability) for he only lived up to his awareness. I want you to live your life on your terms. He said that no one had ever explained this to him before, and he needs to change. He applied himself, done well in treatment and stayed sober for six years that I knew him.

COMMON TERMS

Dry Drunk

The usual dry drunk is someone that claims to be sober after completing a rehab treatment program but shows little, if any, change in behavior. That contemptible, despicable, antisocial attitude and demeanor is still prevalent. The truth is handled very disingenuously, and all manipulations are glaringly exposed. The only thing missing is that drink, which often follows.

Black Out

Temporary loss of consciousness or memory. I personally believe that through the habitual excessive alcoholic consumption, when their life system is suffering from lack of food, sleep, and nutritional support, a portion of the brain becomes anesthetized for a short period of time, resulting in this condition. Often times trying to recall some of the activities of the previous night is impossible.

Rehab

Rehabilitation is the therapeutic process of restoring a person to good mental and physical health. My goal was to always instill a positive motivational piece that could be pulled from the recesses of their minds in time of need for the rest of their lives.

Enabler

One who provides means in any way for the alcoholic to continue their downward slope. One that needs to understand the difference between negative and positive needs.

AA

Alcoholics Anonymous is a group of sober individuals reaching out to assist those in need toward sobriety.

Al-Anon

An organization designed and developed to assist family members and friends understand and cope with a family member with an alcohol problem.

Competency

Is the degree of mastery or ability appropriate to carrying out the professional tasks of an alcoholism counselor.

OEO

Office of Economic Opportunity

HEW

Health Education and Welfare

NIAAA

National Institute Alcohol Abuse and Alcoholism

Prohibition

Prohibition became a real political issue, and in 1917, Congress approved the eighteenth Amendment to the Constitution, which made it unlawful to manufacture, sell, or transport alcoholic beverages within the United States. In 1920 (after ratification by thirty-six states) prohibition became law and remained so until passage of the twenty-first Amendment in 1933.

Moonshiners

Between 1920 and 1933, moonshiners and bootlegers became the providers of most all alcoholic beverages produced in America. To this day, moonshiners with their stills deep in covert mountainous areas, continue production. However, there is stiff prison time if caught.

Responsibility

Responsibility is a relative concept, which involves attitudes based on individual motivation and values. I believe these values are a combination of events that shape our lives from birth to death. It is how we perceive of a given situation for which we find ourselves involved I will not attempt to list all programs in Linn County dealing with alcoholism, but the following two can steer you on a proper course of action.

Area Substance Abuse Council
3601 16th Ave SW
Cedar Rapids, Iowa (319) 390-4611
Alcoholics Anonymous, CR
(319) 365-5955

There is one other program to speak of as I read about in the Gazette, February 24th that begins with offering second chances located in Davenport, Iowa. Place of Refuge Ministries stated goals are to walk with people and assist in the process of restoring, rebuilding, and reconnecting them back to God, family, friends, and their community as spoken by Pastor Tom Thomas and his wife Pastor Stephanie Thomas.

The congregation is comprised of people who have abused various substances, gang members, domestic abuse survivors and abusers both, homelessness, unemployed and underemployed, single-parent families, and ex-offenders.

It seems that whatever is necessary to assist these members in turning their lives around is available. They are equipped with Bible studies, life-skills classes, financial literacy classes, after-school mentoring, counseling, and support groups. They cover the total person without prejudice. They stated that everyone needing a job had one.

AUTHORS NOTE

The names and other details of some major and minor characters have been changed to protect company, individual, privacy and anonymity.

REFERENCES
CMACAO Alcoholism Treatment Program, 1977
National Institute of Alcohol Abuse and Alcoholism 1974
HEW Public Health Service 1974
Reaching the Addicted through Overcomers 1988
The Ohio Alcoholism Counselor Certification Board 1978

ARTISTIC ENDEAVORS
BRIAN C. HEDLUND, MARION, IOWA
and
TAMMY FACION, SWISHER, IOWA

COVID-19 PANDEMIC

Finally a word of encouragement to all Americans affected by COVID-19, continue following the best medical advice daily.

I really want to speak to senior citizens that live alone and may at times over indulge in drink, please be careful as you are on your own, and help is not always readily available. If after repeated episodes, please do not hesitate to make the call for help. Necessary information is found in your phone book or local daily newspaper.

Life is precious, and you only have one on this earth. Let us preserve it as best we can.

PARTICULARS ON SOBRIETY

When we consider all aspects of rehabilitation (rehab), the medical, physical, and psychological portions, plus the social networking process, we are presented with a new lifestyle. The major players are still the program recipients, and they must take complete positive responsibility in their life decisions after discharge.

Now the hard work begins as we are no longer under the umbrella of the in-house monitoring program but are on our own.

If our after-care program includes participation in AA, NA, church, changing friends, hang-outs, key associates, and creating new sober friends, this will impact our desire to stay sober. To maintain sobriety, we must continue in practice what we effectively learned in treatment. We must continually change negative attitudes to positive thought processes in all our ways. Practice does not make perfect, but it does make permanent.

We should always try to regain the positive things that we lost and improve upon whatever we have. We need to stay busy but not over-burdened. Idle minds are not very productive

The dividends of a continuous positive attitude are characteristically those things received from others, though not expected. It is a catalyst for good.

The following statement should be one of our memory guides. Some of us stop the use but never the abuse. Abuse has many faces, from kind manipulation to irrational behavioral instability. Recognize it and flee if you must. This should be a happy time for all, giving back to the larger community that has served them over the years. Remember, be about something positive if at all possible.